Other giftbooks by Helen Exley:
Cat Quotations   Cooks Quotations
Cricket Quotations   Dog Quotations
Friendship Quotations   Golf Quotations
Happiness Quotations   Horse Quotations
Love Quotations   Teddy Bear Quotations
Wine Quotations

Dedication: To my lovely mother, you've given me everything you ever could. This collection says just some of the things I'd like to say in thanks. Helen.

Published in the USA in 1993 by Exley Giftbooks
Published in Great Britain in 1993 by Exley Publications Ltd

12 11 10 9 8 7 6 5 4 3 2 1

Copyright © Helen Exley 1993
Series editor Helen Exley
The moral right of the author has been asserted.

ISBN 1-86187-095-5

A copy of the CIP data is available from the British Library on request.

Edited by Helen Exley.
Pictures researched by Image Select International.
Printed in China.

Exley Publications Ltd, 16 Chalk Hill, Watford, Herts WD1 4BN, United Kingdom.
Exley Publications LLC, 232 Madison Avenue, Suite 1206, NY 10016, USA.

Exley Publications is very grateful to the following individuals and organizations for permission to reproduce their pictures: Atkinson Art Gallery, Southport: page 30; Bonhams, London: page 46; Bridgeman Art Library: cover and pages 6, 7, 14, 22, 57; City of Bristol Museum: pages 52, 53; Christies Colour Library: page 11; Coram Foundation, London: page 55; John Davies Fine Paintings: page 8; © Ditz "Mother and Child": page 34; Fine Art Photographic: pages 24, 28; Mary Evans Picture Library: pages 19, 37; Musee D' Orsay, Paris: pages 12, 13, 44, 45; National Museum, Stockholm: page 16; Oldham Art Gallery: pages 26, 50; Phillips Auctioneers: pages 48, 49; Scala: pages 49,43,59; Turko Art Museum: Page 40; Waterhouse & Dodd, London page 33; Whitford & Hughes, London: page 61; Christopher Wood Art Gallery: pages 20, 21.

*M*OTHER
QUOTATIONS

A COLLECTION
OF BEAUTIFUL PAINTINGS AND
THE BEST MOTHER QUOTES

— ◆ —

A HELEN EXLEY
GIFTBOOK

EXLEY
NEW YORK • WATFORD, UK

"She is their earth .... She is their food and
their bed and the extra blanket when it grows
cold in the night; she is their warmth and
their health and their shelter;...."

KATHERINE BUTLER HATHAWAY

– ◆ –

"A mother always has to think twice, once for
herself and once for her child."

SOPHIA LOREN, b.1934

"When you are a mother, you are never
really alone in your thoughts. You are
connected to your child and to all those
who touch your lives."

SOPHIA LOREN, b.1934

"It's the three pairs of eyes that mothers have
to have....
One pair that see through closed doors.
Another in the back of her head... and,
of course, the ones in front that can look at
a child when he goofs up and reflect
'I understand and I love you' without so
much as uttering a word."

ERMA BOMBECK, b.1927

PROUD AS PUNCH

A mother's children are like ideas; none are
as wonderful as her own.

CHINESE FORTUNE

"My point is that no matter what the
ordinary person says... no matter who it is
that speaks, or what superlatives are
employed, no baby is admired sufficiently to
please the mother."

E. V. LUCAS

"A mother doesn't give a damn
about your looks. *She* thinks you are
beautiful, anyway."

MARION C. GARRETTY, b.1917

"I shall never forget my mother, for it was she who planted and nurtured the first seeds of good within me. She opened my heart to the impressions of nature; she awakened my understanding and extended my horizon, and her percepts exerted an everlasting influence upon the course of my life."

IMMANUEL KANT (1724 - 1804)

— ◆ —

Thou are thy mother's glass, and she in thee
Calls back the lovely April of her prime.

WILLIAM SHAKESPEARE (1564 - 1616)

"They always looked back before turning the
corner, for their mother was always at the
window to nod and smile, and wave her hand
at them. Somehow it seemed as if they
couldn't have got through the day without
that, for whatever their mood might be, the
last glimpse of that motherly face was sure to
affect them like sunshine."

LOUISA MAY ALCOTT (1832 - 1888)

"She brings the sunshine into the house; it is
now a pleasure to be there."

CECIL BEATON (1904 - 1980)

THOUGHTS OF A NEW MOTHER

"Suddenly she was here. And I was no longer
pregnant; I was a mother. I never believed in
miracles before."

ELLEN GREENE

"I love being a mother. I am more aware. I
feel things on a deeper level. I seem to have
more of everything now: more love,
more magic, more energy."

SHELLEY LONG

Thou, straggler into loving arms,
Young climber up of knees,
When I forget thy thousand ways,
Then life and all shall cease.

MARY LAMB (1764-1847)

PROTECTOR

"Everybody knows that a good mother gives
her children a feeling of trust and stability.
Somehow even her clothes feel different to her
children's hands from anybody else's clothes.
Only to touch her skirt or her sleeve makes a
troubled child feel better."

KATHARINE BUTLER HATHAWAY

– ♦ –

"The child, in the decisive first years
of his life, has the experience of his mother,
as an all-enveloping, protective,
nourishing power. Mother is food; she is
love; she is warmth; she is earth. To be loved
by her means to be alive, to be rooted,
to be at home."

ERICH FROMM (1900 - 1980)

– ♦ –

"A mother is a person who if she is not
there when you get home from school
you wouldn't know how to get your
dinner, and you wouldn't feel like
eating it anyway."

ANONYMOUS

— ◆ —

"Now, as always, the most automated appliance in a household is the mother."

BEVERLEY JONES, b.1927

"Any mother could perform the jobs of several air-traffic controllers with ease."

LISA ALTHER

Mother's Wrinkled Hands

Such beautiful, beautiful hands!
Though heart was weary and sad
Those patient hands kept toiling on
That her children might be glad.
I almost weep when looking back
To childhood's distant day!
I think how these hands rested not
When mine were at their play.

UNKNOWN

"We bear the world, and we make it....There was never a great man who had not a great mother - it is hardly an exaggeration."

OLIVE SCHREINER (1855 - 1920)

"Every breath she ever breathed, every effort she ever made, every prayer she ever prayed was for her son....The greatest break that Francis Albert Sinatra ever enjoyed in his entire life, in his entire career, was to have Dolly as a mother."

REVEREND ROBERT PERELLA

"My mother was the most beautiful woman.... All I am I owe to my mother....I attribute all my success in life to the moral, intellectual and physical education I received from her."

GEORGE WASHINGTON (1732 - 1799)

A mother understands what a child
does not say.

JEWISH PROVERB

Mother, I love you so.
Said the child, I love you more than I know.
She laid her head on her mother's arm,
And the love between them kept them warm.

STEVIE SMITH (1902 - 1971)

"To my mother I tell the truth. I have no
thought, no feeling that I cannot share with
my mother, and she is like a second
conscience to me, her eyes like a mirror
reflecting my own image."

WILLIAM GERHARDI (1895 - 1977)

"I would desire for a friend the son who never resisted the tears of his mother."

LACRETELLE

A man loves his sweetheart the most, his wife the best, but his mother the longest.

IRISH PROVERB

"Every man, for the sake of the great blessed Mother in Heaven, and for the love of his own little mother on earth, should handle all womankind gently, and hold them in all honour."

ALFRED, LORD TENNYSON (1809 - 1892)

"That if a man loves his mother he will always love his wife."

GEORGE JEAN NATHAN

"Part of us resents forever the fact that we and
our mothers were closer than we can ever be
to any other creature. They gave us freedom -
but we sense the hidden bond,
and know it's unbreakable."

PAM BROWN, b.1928

"Some are kissing mothers and some
are scolding mothers, but it is love
just the same, and most mothers kiss
and scold together."

PEARL S. BUCK (1892 - 1973)

"That dear octopus from whose tentacles we
never quite escape, nor in our innermost
hearts never quite wish to."

DODIE SMITH (1896 - 1990)

TRUE RICHES

A rich child often sits in a poor
mother's lap.

DANISH PROVERB

Haec Ornamenta Sunt Mea

"Cornelia, the mother of the Gracchi,
once entertained a woman from Campania
at her house. Since the woman made a
great show of her jewels, which were
among the most beautiful of the time,
Cornelia detained her in conversation
until her children came home from
school. Then, pointing to her children,
she said, 'These are my jewels.' "

VALERIUS MAXIMUS 1st Century

"What is truly indispensible for the conduct of life has been taught us by women - the small rules of courtesy, the actions that win us the warmth or deference of others; the words that assure us a welcome; the attitudes that must be varied to mesh with character or situation; all social strategy."

REMY DE GOURMONT (1858 - 1915)

They say that man is mighty,
He governs land and sea,
He wields a mighty sceptre,
O'er lesser powers that be,
But a mightier power and stronger,
Man from his throne has hurled,
For the hand that rocks the cradle,
Is the hand that rules the world.

WILLIAM ROSS WALLACE

"Woman is the salvation or destruction
of the family.
She carries its destinies in the folds of
her mantle."

HENRI-FREDERIC AMIEL (1821 - 1881)

— ◆ —

"In the sheltered simplicity of the first days
after a baby is born, one sees again the
magical closed circle, the miraculous sense of
two people existing only for each other."

ANNE MORROW LINDBERGH, b.1906

"The very word 'Motherhood' has an
emotional depth and significance few terms
have. It bespeaks nourishment and safety and
sheltering arms. It embraces not only the
human state but the animal kingdom - the
tiger fiercely protective of her cubs, the hen
clucking over her brood and spreading her
wings to shield them from the storm. It
speaks of the very beginnings of life in egg or
womb and of nurture in the most critical
stages thereafter."

MARJORIE HOLMES

"In my interest she left no wire unpulled, no stone unturned, no cutlet uncooked."

WINSTON CHURCHILL (1875 - 1965),
on his mother, Jennie Jerome Churchill

"Fifty-four years of love and tenderness and crossness and devotion and unswerving loyalty. Without her I could have achieved a quarter of what I have achieved, not only in terms of success and career, but in terms of personal happiness....She has never stood between me and my life, never tried to hold me too tightly, always let me go free...."

NOEL COWARD (1899 - 1973)

"My mother's love for me was so great that I have worked hard to justify it."

MARC CHAGALL (1889 - 1985),
just before his ninetieth birthday

— ♦ —

"My mother was the making of me. She was so true and so sure of me, I felt that I had someone to live for - someone I must not disappoint. The memory of my mother will always be a blessing to me."

THOMAS A. EDISON (1847 - 1931)

— ◆ —

UNCONDITIONAL LOVE

"Who is it that loves me and will love me for
ever with an affection which no chance, no
misery, no crime of mine can do away?
It is you, my mother."

THOMAS CARLYLE (1795 - 1881),
from a letter to his mother

— ◆ —

"Which one?"
(Dwight D. Eisenhower's mother,
on being asked if she was proud of her son)

— ◆ —

In the eyes of its mother every beetle
is a gazelle.

MOROCCAN PROVERB

— ◆ —

THERE ARE NO POOR MOTHERS

"I got more children than I can rightly take
care of, but I ain't got more than I can love."

OSSIE GUFFY

"All mothers are rich when they love
their children.
There are no poor mothers, no ugly ones,
no old ones.
Their love is always the most beautiful
of the joys."

MAURICE MAETERLINCK (1862 - 1949)

"The real secret behind motherhood...love,
the thing that money can't buy."

ANNA CROSBY

WOMEN KNOW

"The way to rear up children (to be just)
They know a simple, merry, tender knack
Of tying sashes, fitting baby-shoes,
And stringing pretty words
that make no sense,
And kissing full sense into empty words."

ELIZABETH BARRETT BROWNING (1806-1861)

Who ran to help me when I fell,
And would some pretty story tell,
Or kiss the place to make it well?
My Mother.

ANN TAYLOR

"...what do girls do who haven't any mothers
to help them through their troubles?"

LOUISA MAY ALCOTT (1832 - 1888)

"Mother love is the fuel that enables a normal human being to do the impossible."

MARION C. GARRETTY, b.1917

— ♦ —

"Anyone who thinks mother love is as soft and golden-eyed as a purring cat should see a cat defending her kittens."

PAM BROWN, b.1928

— ♦ —

"She broke the bread into two fragments and gave them to the children, who ate with avidity.

'She hath kept none for herself,' grumbled the Sergeant.

'Because she is not hungry,' said a soldier.

'Because she is a mother,' said the Sergeant."

VICTOR HUGO (1802 - 1885)

— ♦ —

"Motherhood is the most emotional experience of one's life. One joins a kind of woman's mafia."

JANET SUZMAN

"Strong, beautiful, happy and successful though her own children may be, somewhere in the inner darkness of a woman's mind lie the recollections of those others, the children, blown away like a flurry of leaves by sickness, sorrow and devilry, by hunger and by war. To have a child is to give her a share in every child and she mourns them as her own."

PAM BROWN, b.1928

"Now that I have these children, I'm just crazed about the world's making it to the next century."

MERYL STREEP, b.1949

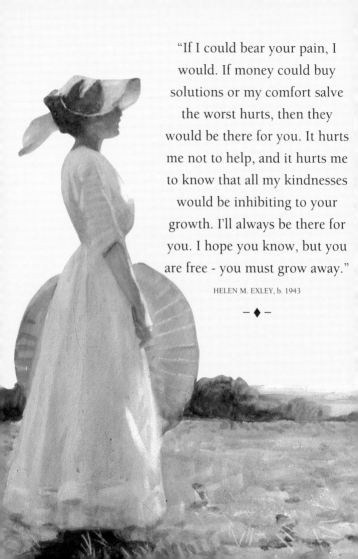

"If I could bear your pain, I would. If money could buy solutions or my comfort salve the worst hurts, then they would be there for you. It hurts me not to help, and it hurts me to know that all my kindnesses would be inhibiting to your growth. I'll always be there for you. I hope you know, but you are free - you must grow away."

HELEN M. EXLEY, b. 1943

– ♦ –

"The everlasting sadness of any mother is that there comes a time when she can no longer bring magic to your life, nor cure to your troubles."

DIANA BRISCOE

— ◆ —

"The older I become, the more I think about my mother."

"It doesn't matter how old I get, whenever I see anything new or splendid, I want to call, 'Mom, come and look'."

"A mother's love for the child of her body differs essentially from all other affections, and burns with so steady and clear a flame that it appears like the one unchangeable thing in this earthly mutable life, so that when she is no longer present it is still a light to our steps and a consolation."

"Mother love makes a woman more vulnerable than any other creature on earth."

PAM BROWN, b.1928

— ◆ —

"What is astonishing, what can give us enormous hope and belief in a future in which the lives of women and children shall be amended and rewoven by women's hands, is all that we have managed to salvage, of ourselves, for our children [...] the tenderness, the passion, the trust in our instincts, the evocation of a courage we did not know we owned, the detailed apprehension of another human existence, the full realization of the cost and precariousness of life. The mother's battle for her child - with sickness, with poverty, with war, with all the forces of exploitation and callousness that cheapen human life - needs to become a common human battle, waged in love and in the passion for survival."

ADRIENNE RICH, b.1929

— ◆ —

REMEMBERING ...

"That lovely voice; how I should weep for joy
if I could hear it now!"

COLETTE (1873-1954)

You too, my mother, read my rhymes
For love of unforgotten times,
And you may chance to hear once more
The little feet along the floor.

ROBERT LOUIS STEVENSON (1850 - 1894)

"The only ghosts, I believe, who creep into
this world, are dead young mothers, returned
to see how their children fare. There is no
other inducement great enough to bring the
departed back."

J. M. BARRIE (1860 - 1937)

LETTING GO

"A mother is not a person to lean on but a person to make leaning unneccessary."

DOROTHY CANFIELD FISHER (1879 - 1958)

"The mother-child relationship is paradoxical and, in a sense, tragic. It requires the most intense love on the mother's side, yet this very love must help the child grow away from the mother and become fully independent."

ERICH FROMM (1900 - 1980)

"My mother wanted me to be her wings, to fly as she never quite had the courage to do. I love her for that. I love the fact that she wanted to give birth to her own wings."

ERICA JONG, b.1942

"Nobody can have the soul of me. My mother
has had it, and nobody can have it again.
Nobody can come into my very self again, and
breathe me like an atmosphere."

D. H. LAWRENCE (1885 - 1930)

"There is an enduring tenderness in the love
of a mother.... It is neither to be chilled by
selfishness, nor daunted by danger,.... She will
sacrifice every comfort to his convenience;
she will surrender every pleasure to his
enjoyment; she will glory in his fame and
exalt in his prosperity; and if adversity
overtake him, he will be the dearer to her by
misfortune; and if disgrace settle upon his
name, she will still love and cherish him; and
if all the world beside cast him off,
she will be all the world to him."

WASHINGTON IRVING (1783 - 1859)